Nine Common Mistakes that Can Wreck Your Auto or Motorcycle Insurance Claim

Avoid These Mistakes to Protect Yourself and Your Family

Louis W. Grande, Esq.

Expert Press

Nine Common Mistakes that Can Wreck Your Auto or Motorcycle Insurance Claim: Avoid These Mistakes to Protect Yourself and Your Family

Louis W. Grande, Esq.
Attorney at Law
395 Smith Street
Providence, Rhode Island 02908
401-351-8000
www.louisgrande.com

ISBN-13: 978-1-946203-15-1
ISBN-10: 1-946203-15-7

Dedication

To Mom and Dad – It's impossible to thank you adequately for everything you've done, from loving me unconditionally to raising me in a stable household, where you instilled traditional values and taught me that anything is possible with faith, hard work, and determination. I could not have been blessed with better parents or role models.

To my brother David – Thank you for all the wonderful memories growing up and for being there when I needed you the most. Your continued support and encouragement are unwavering. I am proud to be called your brother.

A special thank you to my beautiful wife, Sharon, for showering me with patience, kindness, and grace. Your love is a blessing that I am thankful for every day.

For all my loved ones who've gone on to a better place, especially my grandparents, Uncle Nick, and Aunt Kathy – You are always close in heart.

Finally, this dedication would not be complete without a very special thank you to the men and women of the United States military, who protect and defend our freedom all over the world. God bless you!

Contents

Introduction:

How This Book Will Help You and Your Loved Ones Following an Accident

If the idea of a car accident or motorcycle accident horrifies you, know that you are not alone. Accidents of all types, including car accidents, are one of the most common causes of death in the United States.

When your life is already busy and stressful, it is only natural that planning for the worst is not high on your priority list. But knowing what to do—and what not to do—when an accident happens can make all the difference in how it turns out.

It's extremely important to know the mistakes you should avoid. Needless mistakes can jeopardize your ability to receive what you deserve, including fair compensation for any injuries you and your family may have suffered.

I wrote this book to provide you with informative and actionable advice and to help you avoid critical mistakes that can get in the way of receiving the compensation that you deserve.

Car accidents often require long-term medical treatment, and when the accident is fatal, negligent parties must be held accountable for their actions. As a lawyer, I help make this happen for you and your family.

It is also my job as your lawyer to give you the facts and straightforward advice needed to help you make informed decisions.

Allow me to do that by making one thing perfectly clear: The insurance company is not your friend.

There is one recurring theme you'll see throughout this book: Insurance companies are businesses.

Like other businesses, their goal is to keep bringing in more money to earn as much profit as possible. That means that insurance companies, like other businesses, don't like expenses.

Paying money to accident victims (like you and your family members) is an expense. Even when you deserve to be compensated, the insurance companies will do what they can to NOT have to pay for your accident.

That doesn't mean that insurance companies are bad. They are businesses that provide an important service to society. If insurance companies did not exist, there would be no safeguard for you to receive compensation if you get hurt in a car accident when a responsible party is unable to pay.

For example, imagine you are driving home one evening when a drunk driver runs a red light and slams into you at high speed. What if the driver is out of work and can't pay for the significant medical costs that may be needed for you to recover from the accident? In a world without insurance companies, that would be a scary outcome for a driver who was the victim of another driver's negligence.

Fortunately, insurance companies do exist and they provide coverage that pays for the damages you have in an accident. Insurance policies pay for much more than fixing the physical damage to your vehicle.

They also cover policyholders for medical bills, pain and suffering damages, and much more. Even though the insurance company provides a great service, if they have to pay a claim to you, they won't have your best interests at heart when providing this service.

An insurance company that acts like your best friend following an accident does not have your interests at heart.

This book will give you the information you need to avoid the most common mistakes made following an accident.

Let me make another point very clear at the outset of this book: You will almost certainly be entitled to far more compensation than what the insurance company will offer you following an accident.

As mentioned, the insurance company is protecting itself as a business by offering you a lowball amount. It is my job as your lawyer to be the ally who protects your best interests and fights to get you the fair compensation you deserve.

While the insurance company will never be your friend, your lawyer should always be. This is especially true in personal injury law.

The emotional toll an accident takes on families requires more than just capable legal counsel that gets results. It requires compassion and dedication to protect victims and their families and help them receive the compensation they are entitled to by the law.

I have been serving and protecting people just like you for many years, and I can assure you that my legal counsel will help you obtain a much better offer than the one you will get from an insurance company.

Don't accept their initial offer—and you will have already avoided one of the most common mistakes that can sabotage your Rhode Island auto or motorcycle claim.

I want to help you get the most compensation possible since that money is the best way to repair and rebuild your life after a devastating accident that can take both a physical and emotional toll.

This book is designed to do that by helping you avoid the most common mistakes I have seen accident victims make in the days, weeks, and months following an accident.

Without a powerful ally to show you the way, the time following an accident can be stressful and confusing. Whether you are reading this book to learn what to do, or if you have recently been in a car accident in Rhode Island and are looking for helpful information, this book has all of the information that you need.

By avoiding the mistakes outlined in the following chapters, you'll be in a much better position to justify your claim and settle your case for a fair amount that will secure your family's future.

I sincerely hope you and your loved ones will never need to use the information in this book. Vehicle accidents can be unspeakably awful. They have harmed too many Rhode Island families. But it's also an unfortunate truth that I have seen too many avoidable mistakes made by accident victims who did not have all of the information they needed to make the right decisions essential to building a strong case.

Consider this book your resource for the information you need to avoid these mistakes. If you simply avoid these common mistakes, you'll be on your way to getting the compensation you deserve.

If you have any legal questions for me, please call my office. I am always happy to speak with you and provide you with all of the guidance that I can.

Sincerely,
Louis W. Grande, Esq.
Attorney at Law

Mistake #1

Failing to Preserve Evidence at the Scene

The jarring collision of an accident. There's nothing quite as frightening and often life-changing.

You may be injured and you will almost certainly be shaken up following an accident. With the shock of the accident, most people don't think clearly in the moments following. This is especially true for accident victims who find themselves in an accident for the first time.

Knowing What to Do Beforehand Will Help You After an Accident

Being prepared is the best way to guard against feeling helpless and overwhelmed after an accident is knowing what to do beforehand. That knowledge will help you protect yourself and your family if and when an accident happens. To protect yourself, your loved ones, and any future Rhode Island auto or motorcycle claim, it's essential to preserve key evidence at the scene. Failing to do so is often an accident victim's first mistake, and it can harm the outcome of their legal claim.

Witness Information Can Be Key in Building a Strong Legal Claim

Avoid this mistake by making sure to talk to witnesses at the scene of an accident if it is physically possible to do so. If you are hurt badly, receiving immediate medical treatment is most important.

If the injuries are less severe, however, try your best to talk to witnesses in an attempt to obtain key details. Make sure to get the witnesses' contact information: name, address, telephone number, and email if possible. The phone number is the most important information to obtain for a future legal claim.

Sometimes this information is contained in the police accident report, but often it isn't. When you meet with an accident lawyer, you will want to provide them with a phone number that can be used by an investigator who works on behalf of the lawyer. The investigator can then find these witnesses and talk to them about the accident using this information to build a strong case.

Why Visual Evidence of the Accident Scene Matters

If you can get witness contact information, you should also be able to provide visual evidence of the accident scene. You should provide your lawyer with pictures of the vehicles involved in the accident as well as pictures of the streets, traffic signs and lights, and information about the accident scene.

Taking pictures of the vehicles and surrounding areas from every angle will ensure that you are presenting your lawyer with valuable visible evidence that can make a positive difference for your accident claim. If your phone is low on battery life or you are otherwise pressed for time, make sure to at least take photos of the damage to your vehicle and the other vehicles involved in the accident. Also, warning signs, yield signs, and any other traffic control signs can be used to build a stronger case, so take pictures of them as well.

Use the video camera on your smartphone as well. Insurance companies will want evidence showing that the vehicle damage is accurately portrayed and that other facts like the accident time, date, and location are accurate as well.

You can provide all this information in one simple video recorded on your phone. Simply take a video filming the accident surroundings and state your name, the date, time, and accident location.

Continue filming the scene and declare any other information that you may feel is relevant.

This will give you a video filled with valuable, fact-based evidence. The earlier you start using your phone—after checking on your personal safety and the safety of others—the better it is for your accident claim.

Shortly after an accident, vehicles often move before police officers arrive at the accident scene. Without initial photo or video evidence, the circumstances will be harder to prove.

Getting photo or video evidence that a car crossed a double yellow line will prevent a needless, back-and-forth, "he said, she said" battle.

If you are seriously injured, it's far more important that you get the medical treatment you need as quickly as possible, which will help you avoid the second key mistake that can harm your accident claim.

Mistake # 2

Failing to Seek Medical Treatment

Over my many years representing Rhode Island accident victims against insurance companies, I always talk to every one of my clients about the importance of seeking medical treatment as soon as possible. Even if you are only experiencing minor pain or symptoms, it is still important to get medical treatment as soon as you finish collecting evidence at the scene.

Taking Care of Yourself Is the Most Important Way to Help Your Claim

If you already feel you have been injured and you recognize that the injury is serious, seek medical treatment right away—your life could depend on it. In the most serious cases, delayed medical treatment can make your medical condition worse, lead to post traumatic stress disorder (PTSD), and even mask traumatic brain injuries (TBI) that result in death. Simply put, the stakes are too high to forego medical treatment after an accident.

Documented Evidence of Medical Treatment Creates a Stronger Claim

Beyond the obvious importance of taking care of your physical health in the aftermath of an accident, getting medical treatment and documenting it is also essential for your auto or motorcycle accident case. Documentation is always a critically important component of a strong medical case, and this is especially true when you get treated post-accident.

If you wait to seek medical treatment, the insurance company will argue that you were not hurt. Therefore, you should seek medical treatment immediately if you are injured. When you seek medical treatment shortly after an accident, you are given a valuable opportunity to have your medical condition properly documented.

Insurance companies will scour any evidence they can find in the hours, days and weeks after an accident, hoping to find evidence that will undermine your claim. If the insurance company can show that you waited to get medical treatment even though you were injured or that you were generally unconcerned about the potential for injury, they will try to use these facts as justification for paying less than they should for an injury claim.

For this reason, make sure to tell your doctor everything that is hurting you and fully express how you are feeling after the accident.

Documented evidence showing you were in pain shortly after the accident and were not feeling good will support your claim for damages. As I said in the introduction, insurance companies are businesses and they will always try to limit the amount they pay for injury claims.

Failing to get treatment will bolster the insurance company's claim that you were not injured or were not as injured as indicated in your legal claim. The insurance company also might argue that a particular body part was not injured because you did not mention it in your initial doctor's visit.

Understand that You Bear the Legal Burden of Proving an Injury

Our legal system requires accident victims to prove injuries and damages were caused by the negligence of another.

This is an important concept to understand since it supports the idea that you need to always be thinking about the evidence in your case. Having solid evidence is one of the most important things you need to remember.

This is especially true where medical treatment is concerned. I often use the example of a gunshot wound when discussing the importance of treatment with clients. If someone is shot, they will go to the doctor immediately. The same principle should hold true for auto accidents. When you are hurt, go to the doctor!

Don't let insurance companies make the argument that your injury was not all that bad because you waited to see the doctor. Insurance companies can also try to argue that a previously undocumented leg injury—that you failed to tell the doctor about—worsened due to a lack of treatment if you wait a month until finally seeking treatment.

An early medical visit following an accident can make your case. Documented evidence will clearly lay out a case that you were hurt, you promptly saw the doctor, and had a medical professional record your injuries. This is the opposite of an accident victim who tries to be brave and "grin and bear" their injuries. It's clear which of these two accident victims is more likely to be taken advantage of by the insurance company.

Visit a medical professional who is qualified to deal with your injuries after an accident, and you will be well on your way toward avoiding one of the most common accident claim errors.

Mistake #3

Treating the Opposing Insurance Company like a Friend

It may be too strong of a statement to say that you shouldn't cooperate with an opposing insurance company. A better way of putting it is the insurance company is not your friend.

The insurance company has an incentive to pay as little as possible for accident claims. Naturally, then, the insurance company is not your friend, no matter how nice the representative may seem. Your first course of action should be to refer them to your attorney when they call you for the first time.

You may be a nice person and you don't want to be rude or mean. But there is a big difference between not being rude and having a conversation with the insurance company in a way that will harm your case. Let's take a closer look at some of the interactions you absolutely must avoid if you want to prevent the insurance company from minimizing or denying your legal claim.

Avoid Giving a Recorded Statement

f you are truly injured and have nothing to hide, you might think that giving a recorded statement to the insurance company is okay. Nothing could be further from the truth!

The insurance company could use the recorded information against you at a later date. If you have never been in an accident before, you may be wondering why anyone would allow that to happen. Too many accident victims think they need to answer to the other party's insurance carrier. They give the insurance company more authority in their mind than the company actually has legally.

Insurance companies may talk tough or try to come across as authoritative when they say you need to provide a recorded statement about the facts of an accident. Despite their bluster and bravado, most of the time there is no legal requirement for an accident victim to provide a recorded statement after an accident in Rhode Island.

Just don't do it. You can still treat the company respectfully with your denial. The insurance company would listen to your statement while actively searching for any and all inconsistencies that would support their position and undermine yours.

Recorded Statements Get Distorted and Taken Out of Context

For a great example of this, watch a famous legal scene from the classic legal comedy *My Cousin Vinny*. The movie centers around a murder. The defendant, a college student is being questioned after being falsely arrested for killing a clerk at a grocery store. The college student is shocked since he thought his arrest was for accidentally stealing a can of tuna from the store. After he realizes the local sheriff believes he murdered the clerk, the student responds in disbelief, "I shot the clerk?"

At trial, this response from the student defendant is delivered in a deadpan, affirmative tone, the sheriff making it sound as if it was the young man's confession. "He said, 'I shot the clerk.'"

While this example comes from a comic movie, the same type of misinterpretation can happen if you give a recorded statement to the insurance company. Imagine the insurance company asks you how you are feeling. You decide to respond politely as you would to a friend. "Oh, I'm okay," you respond, not wanting to sound like a complainer. You know you are in pain, but you have the personality to tough things out and stay positive. For the insurance company, however, you just provided evidence that can be distorted and taken out of context—just like the *My Cousin Vinny* example.

The insurance company is looking to take statements like this out of context if it helps limit the amount of compensation you receive. The fact is, it's too early and premature to discuss how you are feeling anyway. Don't give the insurance company a chance to distort your claim: Refuse their attempts to get a recorded statement.

Do Not Sign a Medical Release

Sign a medical release upon the insurance company's request, and the end result is that they may be able to gain access to your entire medical history!

Medical release forms that the insurance company will want you to sign are often broad in scope and not limited in time. The insurance company may request medical reports going back 10 years, and they may try to use the information to justify limiting a claim from the accident.

Suppose you have previously suffered with back pain from a fall 10 years ago. Even if your back has been fine for 10 years, the insurance company could try to use this information to minimize the payout for back injuries caused by the auto accident.

Do not sign anything from the opposing parties' insurance company. This rule is especially true for a general medical release form. If you do not yet have a lawyer, the insurance company may try to pressure you in an attempt to have you sign. Avoid their strong-arm tactics by refusing to sign, and then contact to a Rhode Island auto and motorcycle accident lawyer as quickly as possible.

Don't Limit the Damages to Which You Are Entitled

In an accident claim, you will be entitled to compensation for medical bills, property damage from the accident, and lost time from work. Insurance companies may try to use this to their advantage by convincing you that these are the only damages to which you are entitled. In many cases, this is wrong.

The insurance company won't go out of its way to tell you about pain and suffering or special damages you may be entitled to receive. If your accident results in a scar, you may even be entitled to money for that. Since insurance companies have a duty to maximize profits for their shareholders, these damages and others like them will not be mentioned.

This is part of their strategy to lowball the offer in the hopes that you sign off and agree to a lesser amount than what you are legally entitled to receive. When you are an accident victim, and you need money, it is tempting to take the first offer you receive. However, a quick settlement is often in the best interest of the insurance company, not you.

Don't Sell Yourself Short by Settling Prematurely.

Make it a point to contact an accident lawyer who can help you quickly gauge the magnitude of your injuries while investigating the facts of the case. You deserve more than what the insurance company wants you to believe an accident claim is worth, and the best way to receive the compensation you deserve is by letting your lawyer fight for a fair settlement on your behalf.

11:45 pm
Social

Mistake # 4

Posting to Social Media

While the mistakes in this book are not ranked in order of importance, posting to social media deserves an early mention because of how important it is.

There will soon be more than 2 billion monthly active users on Facebook, so it's clear that social media has forever changed the way we communicate. Less obvious, but more important for your accident claim, is the fact that social media has given insurance companies a new way to undermine your accident claim.

Slate's "Evidence of Life on Facebook" provides an excellent look at how social media has been used to undermine an accident victim's legal claim. One of the examples was a case where the emotional state of a victim on social media was used to actively undermine her claim. The woman's car was rear-ended while she drove to work, so she sued the man who caused the accident.

The woman claimed she was left with chronic pain and a loss of enjoyment of life. In addition, she also argued she could no longer dance with family like she was used to doing and could no longer wrestle and roughhouse with her brother. Her claims were significantly undermined when Facebook pictures revealed her happily dancing and being lifted into the air by her brother soon after the accident!

The woman said that the pictures were fake, but the judge said that whether they were fake or real did not matter. All that mattered was the photographs provided proof that the pictures were taken in an active social setting in a way that demonstrated the accident victim was enjoying life, thereby harming her claim stating she was left with "a loss of enjoyment of life." Examples like these put a real-world face on the fact that what you post on social media can and will wreck your accident claim if you are not careful.

Here are a few ways social media can harm your accident case if you do not implement wise social media practices over the duration of your case.

The Insurance Company May Try to View Your Accounts

Your social media profiles are a potential treasure trove of information for the insurance company to access and undermine your claim.

- What have you been doing since your injury or disability?
- Have you been enjoying life just a bit too visibly to justify pain and suffering damages?

These are the types of questions an insurance company will try to ask if they gain access to your profile. This new area of defense, as the Slate article shows, has been used to a good degree of success in recent years at trial.

Social media posts, pictures, and videos are now a potential weapon to be used against you. In fact, even the social media pages of friends can be used against you!

The *Slate* article also told the story of a plaintiff who claimed she was wrongly terminated as a manager at Home Depot, and was socially isolated from her friends as a result of the termination. The opposing counsel successfully argued that dozens of "Happy Birthday!" messages on Facebook from friends showed that she was not actually socially isolated.

Of course, this was not an accident case. But it does show that the most innocent social media posts like birthday greetings can be used to harm your claim.

Suppose that a friend finds out that you were in an auto accident and asks how you are feeling. As mentioned earlier, imagine you just want to make the best of a bad situation by telling them, "I'm okay."

An insurance company or opposing counsel that accesses that information will use it and attempt to distort it into demonstrating that your injuries are not as serious as you claim. Think back to the My Cousin Vinny example cited in the section on Mistake #3, and you are on the right track.

Don't let social media posts get distorted in a way that raises doubt in a jury's mind. Doubt about whether you are truly hurt can be the make-or-break difference in your case. There are no do-overs for social media mistakes.

Programs and software exist today that allow users to retrieve information that was previously deleted.

As a general rule, it is best to simply stay off of social media until your case is resolved. Here are five valuable social media tips and best practices that will benefit your auto or motorcycle claim.

Social Media Tip # 1: Update Privacy Settings

If your profile is public, everything on your account is fair game to prying eyes. This can spell disaster for your case. The most important thing you can do if you have not done so already is to limit access to your social media accounts by making them private.

Insurance companies and opposing lawyers will have a difficult time using social media against you if they have to work harder to see the pictures and information you post.

Opposing counsel will have a hard time justifying a subpoena request to access your private account information, whereas public profiles are the easiest thing in the world to access.

Social Media Tip # 2: Download Complete Records of Your Accounts

One thing insurance companies or opposing counsel may try to do is claim they have social media evidence that harms your case. This tactic can be used to get you to accept a lower offer than you deserve.

Don't fall for the trap. Prepare in advance by downloading hard copies of your social media account. Having physical records will help you dispute false claims with hard evidence.

Social Media Tip # 3: Adopt a Policy of Silence for All Things Case-Related

If you follow only one social media tip, make it this one. Do not talk about your case at all online, not even with your best friend via private messages.

Posting updates and opinions about the case is also a poor decision, and it is unnecessary. Let your attorney advise you on legal matters, and don't share what your lawyer said to you on social media. This can tip off opposing counsel or the insurance company, needlessly giving them more time to counter the arguments that favor you.

Your family will want updates, but limit those to in-person conversations.

Social Media Tip # 4: Ask Friends and Family to be Silent

Well-meaning friends and family can do far more damage on social media than an insurance company or opposing counsel. You need to make sure your friends and family don't harm your case by discussing it on social media. Also, understand that your friends can tag you in posts that show what you are doing or where you are.

This is valuable information for an insurance company. If you have been jet skiing after claiming serious leg injuries and back pain, a tagged post from a friend can seriously jeopardize your right to deserved compensation.

Let your friends know in advance not to talk about your case online or tag you/share photos of you until the case is resolved.

Social Media Tip # 5: Talk to Your Lawyer Before Deleting Information

While you need to be careful about your social media use, don't overreact and delete all your accounts and posts before talking to your accident lawyer.

There may be an ethical duty to preserve evidence if you or your friends have already talked about the case. Your lawyer can help you minimize the fallout of any mistakes without adding ethical violations on top of them.

Doing so will needlessly harm your case. It's best if you stay off social media altogether, but always keep your lawyer informed so he or she can help you avoid any roadblocks or needless issues that can and will hurt your case.

While on the subject of discussing issues with your lawyer in complete transparency, failing to be honest in conversations is another common mistake that can ruin your case.

Medical
Record
Name
Date

Mistake #5

Withholding Information

As discussed earlier, the most important thing you can do for your case is gather evidence. You also shouldn't do anything that harms the evidence you gather or do anything that gives the insurance company evidence to use against you.

These same principles hold true when it comes to withholding information from your lawyer or medical providers. If your medical reports are based on inaccurate information because you didn't mention everything when you spoke with the doctor, your case can be ruined.

If you lie to your lawyer about the facts and the lawyer relies on those statements to create a strong case, that will also ruin your claim.

Medical and legal professionals provide the most help to you and your accident claim, so always be completely truthful with them. You should also never withhold information from them.

Withholding information can be just as destructive to your claim as lying. Let's walk through a couple of hypothetical scenarios to illustrate how withholding information could hurt you.

Withholding Information from Your Doctor

Imagine you are in a great deal of pain and you decide to visit your doctor or medical provider. Using the customary 1-to-10 pain scale rating, suppose that your back is a "10" on a pain level (the worst), but you also have knee pain that rates at a "2" on the pain level (discomfort) on your first visit.

When your doctor asks you to list everything that hurts, you say that your back is in a lot of pain. The doctor asks follow-up questions, making notes on exactly where the pain is and what body part is injured based on what you say. You don't mention the knee pain since it's relatively minor.

A few weeks pass, and the pain in your back has gotten better. Unfortunately, the pain in your knee has increased quite dramatically (say, from a "2" to a "7"). You schedule another visit to the doctor and tell him about the knee pain this time, weeks after the accident. The doctor will ask follow-up questions and take notes regarding your knee pain.

This may seem like no big deal, but the insurance company will argue that something happened AFTER the accident because you didn't mention it when you were seen even though you had mild pain when you were there initially. It's easy to believe that the knee injury happened in the weeks between doctor visits.

Remember that the burden is on you to prove that an accident caused your injuries. Withholding information like this that can be used to provide the evidence your case will need is unwise.

The best way to prevent this from being an issue is to discuss every ailment you are suffering openly and honestly. Even if the pain is minor, mention it to the doctor while stating honestly that the pain is minor. The doctor will take note of that, which will show documented evidence that the pain existed immediately after the accident should the ailment worsen over time, which is not uncommon in auto and motorcycle accidents.

Withholding Information from Your Lawyer

Just as withholding information from your doctor is a mistake, so is withholding information from your injury attorney. You must discuss absolutely everything with your lawyer if you expect them to be able to provide you with the best legal advice and counsel.

If you have pre-existing conditions, you need to disclose them to both your lawyer and doctor. An injury from a previous motorcycle accident, boating accident, or sports injury may be relevant to your case. The earlier your lawyer has the full picture and all the information, the more time the attorney will have to create the strongest possible legal argument.

It's tempting not to disclose this information, but trust me when I tell you that the news will get to the insurance company. In my more than 28 years of courtroom litigation experience, I can't recall an instance where all the relevant medical information did not come to light. Part of the reason for this is that insurance companies use claims registries to check information concerning prior accidents.

When the truth comes out regarding an undisclosed former injury in the same spot you are now claiming was injured in your current accident, you will look dishonest. Even if your lawyer is somehow able to overcome that appearance of deception, it's likely that the value of your accident case will be harmed. <u>Honesty is not only the best policy for an auto accident claim; it is the only policy</u> if you are serious about receiving the compensation you and your loved ones deserve.

Don't believe that you need to hide information in order to protect your legal claim.

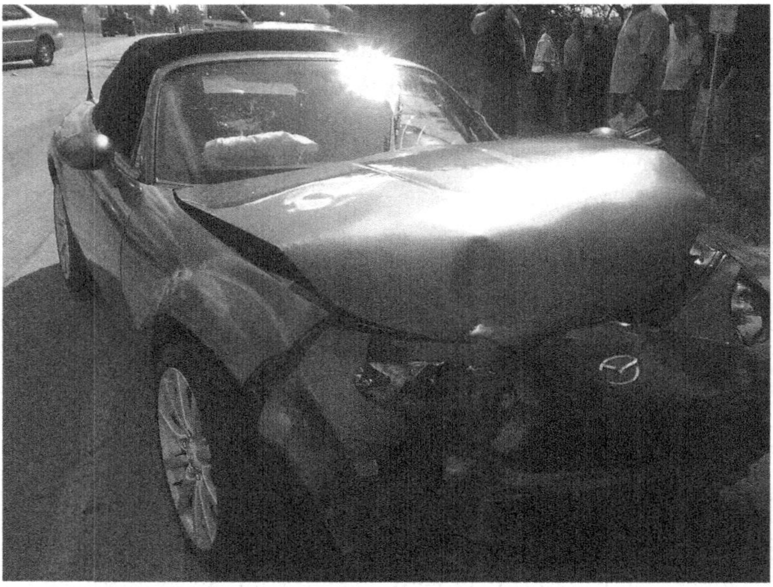

Mistake #6

Believing that You Have No Claim

One of the worst mistakes you can make after an accident is believing that you have no legal claim to compensation. Whether you think this because you have a pre-existing condition (causing you to withhold information as discussed in the previous chapter) or you think that the facts are stacked against you, don't you believe it!

The worst thing you can do is give up before you contact an attorney. Many personal injury lawyers operate under a fee structure that says the lawyer will not get paid for their services or counsel unless they recover money for you.

That means it's always worth contacting a lawyer to find out whether you have a claim or another path toward getting compensation for your injuries. It costs you nothing, and you could potentially gain compensation. Make the phone call.

The insurance company is happy when you throw in the towel based on a belief that you have no claim. That works to their advantage, and in fact, they may be the one trying to sell you on that idea.

Don't let them do it; call a lawyer.

When the Insurance Company Denies a Claim

If there are no witnesses at the scene of your accident, don't be surprised if the insurance company uses the lack of witnesses as a reason for denying liability based on the statement of the other party.

If you get into an accident with another driver and there are no witnesses, the other driver may say that they were not at fault. If the driver makes a signed statement to that effect, then the insurance company may deny liability for your injuries.

If you think that the other driver and the insurance company are not liable, they may convince you to simply give up and walk away.

If an accident victim gives up on a claim, the insurance company may save up to thousands of dollars in payouts. Don't let that be you!

Another common reason that accident victims give up on a claim is when both drivers were at fault in some way. Legally, this is known as joint tortfeasors, meaning both parties are at least partially responsible for the accident. If you give up on your claim because you were partly to blame, you may be needlessly throwing away the possibility of receiving compensation.

Rhode Island law gives you the potential to recover compensation in an auto or motorcycle accident, even if you are partly at fault.

Rhode Island uses a pure joint liability standard known as the pure comparative fault rule. This rule simply means that your fault will be used to reduce the amount of compensation you receive, based on the percentage of your fault. If the other driver was far more at fault than you (say, 75 percent responsible to your 25 percent), you could still be entitled to a substantial amount of compensation. Again, call a Rhode Island accident lawyer and talk about your case before giving up. You have nothing to lose.

Denying Claims Based on Lack of Coverage

Another typical claim denial that can lead an accident victim to give up occurs when the insurance company denies the claim based on a lack of insurance coverage. Even if the at-fault party does not have insurance, you may still be able to collect under your own insurance policy if you have uninsured motorist coverage.

Uninsured motorist coverage is defined as coverage that protects the policyholder in the event that the other driver is legally responsible for the accident but is not insured. Rhode Island auto insurance companies are legally required to offer uninsured motorist coverage, but you can decline it if you wish. It can be very beneficial to have this coverage, however, based on the number of uninsured drivers in Rhode Island.

According to recent data from the Insurance Research Council, 17 percent of Rhode Island drivers are uninsured, which is the eighth-highest percentage in the country. For this reason, I always advise friends, family and clients alike to get uninsured motorist coverage. Even though Rhode Island law requires motorists to have liability insurance coverage, too many drivers are ignoring the law.

But even if another driver doesn't have liability insurance and you don't have uninsured motorist coverage, the other driver may still have enough assets to satisfy an award to cover your injuries.

The fact that an insurance company denies liability or coverage does not mean that you have no legal claim or an alternative path to recovering the compensation you deserve.

As you can see, it is important to call a lawyer as soon as possible. Waiting to hire an attorney is another common mistake that can wreck your case because you are essentially flying blind without the sound legal advice of a personal injury lawyer.

Mistake # 7

Waiting to Hire an Attorney

If you have had experience dealing with insurance companies before, you know that they play hardball. Insurance adjusters process claims every day for a living. An accident is new and uncharted territory for most people.

Why face an experienced insurance professional by yourself? As soon as you have collected evidence at the scene and talked to witnesses, you need to take care of your physical health by visiting a doctor. The very next step should be retaining the services of an auto and motorcycle accident lawyer who will fight for the compensation you deserve.

Your Injury Lawyer is Your Ally

Just as the insurance company fights these battles every day, so does your personal injury lawyer. The lawyer is your advocate and ally who fights in the trenches against insurance companies on a daily basis, helping injured victims just like you receive the fair offers you deserve. Every trick an insurance company tries to play is best countered with proven legal strategies and actions based on the counsel of a Rhode Island lawyer who understands Rhode Island personal injury laws.

Mistakes Your Lawyer Will Help You Avoid

If you hire a lawyer early on in the process, he or she will help keep you from making mistakes. Giving a recorded statement, signing a medical release, or talking about the case on social media are all things your lawyer will warn you about.

All of these mistakes can hurt the value of your claim, and finding a good lawyer is your best safeguard against making them. Your lawyer will not get paid until you do, and the offer you will receive is likely to be higher than an offer you might receive if you try to represent yourself. Why is that? You don't have the benefit of legal education and years of experience handling insurance claims.

For example, if you have to take a couple weeks off to recover before returning to work, those two weeks off can count as lost wages for which you can receive compensation. This is standard information to a practicing personal injury lawyer, but an accident victim would have no reason to know that if this is the first accident they've been in.

They may not know to track their time off work for recovery or time taken off to visit the doctor, but your lawyer will tell you about all the steps you can take to help maximize your compensation. Such small steps may not be obvious at first glance. Your lawyer will help you avoid not only major mistakes but also these small mistakes.

Mistake #8

Accepting an Initial Offer

If you hire an attorney early in the process, you will avoid the mistake of accepting an initial offer from an insurance company. A first settlement offer from the insurance company is almost certainly a lowball offer, and it is not one you want to take.

Remember our mantra: An insurance company is a business whose model is designed to prevent high payouts to victims.

The initial offer is no good, and the insurance company knows it. Thanks to this book and the advice of your lawyer, now you know it too.

There are many factors that go into receiving a fair offer following an auto or motorcycle accident. For example:

- Is there a possibility or even a certainty of future lost wages?
- Could future injuries be so serious that it is possible the individual will never work again?
- If so, how could such an accident victim possibly have an understanding of how the legal system could compensate for such a horrific and serious accident?

A lawyer, on the other hand, will have the knowledge and experience necessary to understand the value of the case.

This expertise is essential, especially when there are long-term injuries or even permanent disabilities. When you may have future medical costs, treatments, and future pain and suffering, it's nearly impossible to know what your claim is worth without talking to a lawyer.

Even if an insurance company's offer seems like a lot of money now, you may end up realizing that they shortchanged you with a lowball offer when you run out of money for medical treatments years later.

Future considerations can be difficult to take into account when you and your loved ones need money now. But this natural urge to receive money right away is precisely what the insurance company is counting on. Fight this urge, and you will be far better off for having done so.

Why Waiting for the Settlement You Deserve is the Right Choice

Signing a release that is based on an offer that is too low is a permanent choice. You do not get a second chance. That's why it's so important to get the settlement right the first time.

If injuries worsen over time or the injuries were not properly investigated before you settle, you and your loved ones may not even know the full scope of what you just agreed on upon.

What may have been a soft tissue injury at the time of settlement may turn out to become a herniated disc that requires extensive treatment. You need to understand the extent of your medical condition before your case is settled.

Accepting an early offer makes it difficult for you to properly assess your potential damages. That means the insurance company will never provide an offer to cover those potential damages because a thorough investigation has not yet brought those facts to light.

Expect the insurance company to make the offer sound appealing while impressing upon you how urgent it is to resolve the matter. The reality is that the more thorough the investigation, the more likely it is that the insurance company will actually pay out a <u>fair</u> offer.

Insurance companies do not want you to hire an attorney, for obvious reasons. Claims that settle with a lawyer bring in more money for accident victims, and insurance companies know this. It is in their best interest to rush to provide you with an offer that seems so fair that you question the need to even consult a lawyer.

You owe it to yourself and your loved ones to slow down, take a step back, and make a quick phone call to a lawyer you can count on. If you are reluctant to make that call after an accident, it might be because you think the claim will drag on for years. Fortunately, that is rarely the case.

Your lawyer should serve as trusted counsel who provides you with all the information you need to make an informed decision. If you ever decide that the time is right to settle and you are tired of waiting, that is your decision to make. That said, you will almost certainly receive a better offer after your lawyer has investigated your case and fought the insurance company on your behalf.

Most claims are resolved quickly once you have finished your medical treatment and there is a more complete understanding of the total short- and long-term medical costs, lost wages, and any special damages.

There is a reason most auto accident cases settle out of court. I estimate that roughly 97 percent of the accident cases I have handled have been settled. With more than 28 years of experience at all levels of the federal and state court system, I can assure you that the reason my cases don't go to court is that I get the insurance company to deliver a fair offer.

If they don't, I take the case to trial.

The final decision is yours to make. If you are ready to settle, you can do so. A swift and fair resolution is possible if you have a bit of patience and put your case in the hands of a Rhode Island lawyer who can take the fight to the insurance company on your behalf. If you are concerned about the time waiting for compensation, simply ask your lawyer for more information about the expected timeline. Your lawyer should provide you with timely case updates and should have at least some general notion of how long the case should take to resolve.

Mistake #9

Limiting the Role of the Police in Your Case

After a car or motorcycle accident in Rhode Island, you can usually count on the familiar sound of sirens indicating that the police are on their way. If the police do not arrive, however, do not think you have gotten lucky.

No matter what your past experience has been with the police, know that they are there to help. When police arrive, they are going to want to fill out a police report.

Without a police report or a police presence at all, you will be forced to count on the other driver if they were at fault and no other witnesses are present. A driver may act friendly and suggest that you resolve differences without bringing the police into the picture.

That may sound like a good deal if you want to get on with your day. Doing so, however, leaves you without important evidence that builds a stronger case for you.

Why You Need to Call the Police

Even if the accident is minor, having the police show up will help prevent a driver from changing their story from what they initially said.

Rhode Island law requires you to contact the police after an accident occurs. The other driver may have all sorts of valid reasons for not wanting the police, and perhaps you do as well. You are still required to contact the police after an accident.

Some of the reasons police presence may not be desired include:

- A driver is operating their vehicle with a suspended license.
- The driver doesn't want insurance rates to increase.
- The driver is one of the 17 percent of Rhode Island drivers who are driving without auto insurance.

Whatever the reason, understand that it's a big risk for your accident claim if you choose not to call the police. Another driver could later say you caused the accident and sue you for injuries that you were not responsible for. If there are no witnesses, it can come down to their word against yours.

This can be an added cost and source of stress nobody should be forced to deal with after an accident it's the risk drivers take when they decide the police are not needed following an accident.

The most important reason for calling the police to the accident scene is to create an unbiased record of the facts about the accident.

The Importance of the Police Report

When police arrive at the scene of the accident, they will complete and file a police report. If it doesn't look like they will be filing a report, for whatever reason, be bold and request that they do so. It's highly unlikely that they won't, though, as police officers are trained to file these reports and to conduct a proper accident investigation.

To understand why the police report is so important requires understanding what is included in a standard police report. The typical police report in a Rhode Island car accident includes key details like basic contact information of all parties in the accident and a description of what occurred at the scene after conducting an investigation.

The scope of the investigation depends on the nature of the accident. If the accident was a minor fender-bender, expect the report investigation to be fairly minor so the officer can move on to more pressing public safety issues. As an accident scales in either severity or criminality (such as a DUI), you can expect an increasingly in-depth police report. For complex accident scenes, the police report can be one of the most valuable pieces of evidence you will have in a fight against the insurance company.

Either way, the report typically involves locating accident parties and as well as witnesses, and recording important information to be provided by these individuals. The officer may then make their own conclusions based on their observations about what may have contributed to or caused the accident.

The report may also diagram the event and the accident scene, noting where traffic signals and important accident factors were located related to the crash site. Finally, the report will include claims from drivers involved if they state that the accident was caused by faulty equipment, such as a defective brake in their car. The officer will likely record such a claim and report it to relevant Rhode Island authorities.

Putting the Police Report to Good Use

It should be plain to see that the police report can provide a great deal of evidence that can build a strong case against the insurance company.

Since you need to prove your injuries were caused by an at-fault party to recover compensation, not getting a police report is one of the worst mistakes you can make, yet it's one that is all too common.

Providing the police report to an insurance claims adjuster will speed up the claims process. Getting through one key roadblock faster is an important benefit in itself, but your lawyer will also put a police report to good use when building your case.

Ways Your Lawyer Can Use the Police Report

A police officer's observations in the report may indicate who is at fault, which can be a huge benefit to your case when dealing with the insurance company. If the other driver is clearly at fault, the insurance company may want to settle quickly in order to avoid the costs of litigation when it is clear they will need to pay up. You may be wondering what this means if the officer's report indicates that you are at fault.

Even if you were partially at fault and that is reflected in the report, we have already discussed how partial fault does not bar you from receiving compensation in Rhode Island.

Regardless of fault or other worries you might have, the police report is going to be a valuable piece of evidence that can help you at trial. Don't be scared into thinking that most cases need to go to trial. As I have mentioned previously, about 97 percent of the cases that I have handled have settled without the need for a trial.

That said, cases that go to trial tend to be complex, and you need to prove your case with evidence. In a complex case, a favorable police report can tilt the balance in your favor when used along with the testimony of an officer who was on the scene.

Additionally, if you were in serious condition and could not photograph evidence at the scene or talk to witnesses as we discussed when reviewing Mistake #1, the accident report may be the best piece of documented evidence your lawyer will have.

Summary

You now have the knowledge to avoid nine of the most common mistakes that wreck auto and motorcycle accident claims. These mistakes have ruined cases, but more often they reduce the deserved compensation you and your loved ones should have been able to count on while taking steps to repair, restore, and rebuild your lives following an accident.

Avoid These Mistakes and More: Choose the Right Accident Lawyer

As a personal injury lawyer, I wrote this book because I care about my clients and their families. Allow me to say a few parting words about why choosing the right lawyer for your accident in Rhode Island is the best choice you can make.

In a book focused on mistakes, it could be said that choosing the wrong lawyer for your case is a mistake in and of itself. As a personal injury lawyer with many years of experience, I think it is best said that choosing the right lawyer is the best decision you can make.

The lawyer you choose will help you avoid these nine common mistakes and many less common errors. But more importantly, you will know you have an ally in your corner who is always looking out for your best legal interests and the interests of your loved ones.

Choosing the Right Lawyer for Your Case

The right lawyer is one who can promise to provide the following:

- Compassion and Commitment
- Avoidance of Mistakes
- Reliable Results
- Effective Advocacy

Taken on the whole, this helpful acronym can be simplified into saying you need a lawyer who exhibits CARE.

Compassion and Commitment

You and your loved ones have been through a great ordeal after an accident, and nobody (not even an injury lawyer) is capable of grasping the difficulties you and your family face.

A lawyer should give your case the care and compassion it deserves. Tragic accidents are shocking and transformative, two factors a caring attorney needs to keep in mind from Day One of the case until its close.

Some days you may be exhausted by doctor visits. Other days, you may be stressed about winning the claim. Your lawyer should shoulder the load with you, giving you the confidence that your case is in good hands.

While being able to win the case is the most important part of being a personal injury lawyer, from my experience I can say that genuine concern for a client's emotional health and physical wellbeing ranks as a close second.

Avoiding Mistakes

I wrote this book because I have seen accident victims make too many mistakes that harm cases. I have more than 28 years of courtroom litigation experience, and I am proud to say that my time in personal injury law has led to my being recognized as one of the Top 100 Rhode Island Trial Lawyers by the National Trial Lawyers Association.

As my track record demonstrates, I have helped accident victims avoid mistakes that can needlessly harm their case. I will not let the insurance company get away with lowballing you based on avoidable mistakes or technicalities.

Reliable Results

When I represent a new client, I get to work cutting through the red tape and the lowball settlement offers to get the results accident victims deserve.

When I work on behalf of my clients, I never take shortcuts, and I am proud to say that my record shows that I produce winning results for my clients and their families.

You get results that you can count on. My clients are informed and they know what to expect as the case progresses. Prompt communication and timely case updates are the best ways I know to put accident victims at ease during this difficult time. I also give my clients an honest assessment of their claim.

I produce results that have helped countless Rhode Island families live better lives because they receive the compensation they deserve.

Effective Advocacy

Finally, the right lawyer for your case will be capable of advocating effectively on your behalf.

What do I mean by effective advocacy? It's my job to communicate and effectively argue with insurance companies and the judge and jury at trial. My 28 years of experience advocating for the rights of Rhode Island accident victims demonstrate a track record of success.

If you are receiving a lowball offer, you will hear it from me first. If I think the offer is fair, I'll let you know that as well. To make an informed and empowered legal decision, you need to fully understand your options since the legal decision is yours to make.

No matter what choice you make, the right lawyer will be with you each step of the way until the claim is resolved.

Final Thoughts

It is my sincere hope that this book and these parting words have given you the information you need to avoid mistakes and choose the right lawyer who will help you avoid even the most difficult-to-spot mistakes.

And yes, it's my hope that after reading this book and contacting me, I will earn the right to represent you or your loved ones after a Rhode Island auto or motorcycle accident.

I hope this book has been of great value to you and has given you the confidence that I am the right Rhode Island auto and motorcycle accident lawyer for your case.

As the term "personal injury law" implies, I believe it should be precisely that: personal.

I look forward to discussing the facts of your case and making it my personal mission to help you and your loved ones receive the compensation you need to establish a sense of normalcy in your life once again.

Please don't hesitate to reach out to me for a legal consultation after reading this book if you are ready to take the first steps toward resolving your legal claim with the insurance company. I look forward to speaking with you.

About the Author

Louis W. Grande is the founding member of the Grande Law Firm.

The Grande Law Firm is a personal injury law firm dedicated to fighting aggressively for the rights of injured victims involved in automobile and motorcycle accidents. Mr. Grande is admitted to practice law in Rhode Island and before the United States District Court. He has appeared and successfully argued before courts at the local, state, and federal levels.

He is a member of the Rhode Island Association for Justice, Rhode Island Bar Association, Top 25 Motor Vehicle Accident Attorneys, Top 100 Trial Lawyers, and the Municipal Court Judges Association.

He was presented the Pro Bono Publico Award by the Rhode Island Bar Association for providing free legal services to the less fortunate. He is a graduate of LaSalle Academy, the honors program at Rhode Island College, and the Hamline University School of Law where he was the primary editor of the *Journal of Law and Public Policy*.

Mr. Grande aggressively fights on a daily basis for injured victims and currently serves as an Associate Municipal Court Judge for the town of Lincoln, Rhode Island.

Louis W. Grande, Esq.
Attorney at Law
395 Smith Street
Providence, Rhode Island 02908
401-351-8000
www.louisgrande.com

Sources

http://www.cbsnews.com/news/the-leading-causes-of-death-in-the-us/

https://www.fool.com/investing/2017/03/30/how-many-users-does-facebook-have.aspx

http://www.slate.com/articles/technology/users/2015/04/social_media_and_the_law_if_you_re_claiming_emotional_distress_don_t_appear.html

http://www.m-n-law.com/legal-services/auto-accident-lawyer/

http://www.carinsurance.com/Articles/uninsured-motorist-coverage-state-averages-of-uninsured-drivers.aspx

http://www.autodamageexperts.com/diminished-value/faq/

Expert
Press

www.ExpertPress.net

Made in the USA
Monee, IL
04 November 2026

67387201R00036